Making Art with Light

Jonathon Phillips
Photographs by Lindsay Edwards

Contents

Light and Art

Light is vital to life on Earth. Sunlight provides warmth and helps plants and animals grow. On a dark night, a light can help people to see, or guide them to safety. In the past, sailors used the stars to **navigate** their ships across the seas.

The three art activities in this book focus on light. The first two activities include colour, but light is needed to see the colours properly. The final activity involves making a black artwork, and light is used to show the picture.

A Beautiful Lantern

A lantern-lit walk in the dark can be a fun and magical thing to do on a still evening. Family and friends go for a long walk outdoors, and everyone carries a lantern to light the way. This lantern is made out of paper, but they can also be made from bottles, jars or milk cartons.

Goal

To make a simple, colourful lantern

Materials

You will need:

a few sheets of newspaper

wax crayons

two sheets of baking paper, about 30 cm wide and 40 cm long

a grater

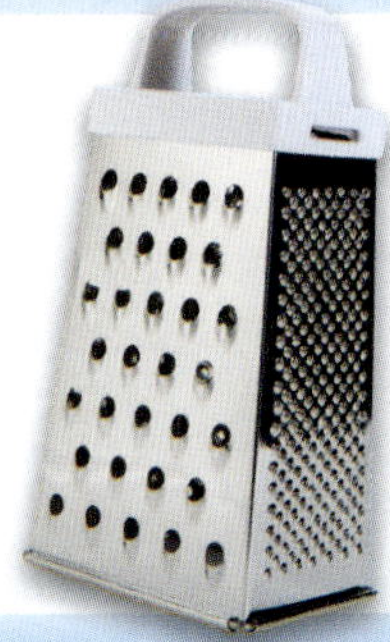

an iron

glue

a small bowl

a stapler

a small piece of cardboard

an LED tealight candle.

scissors

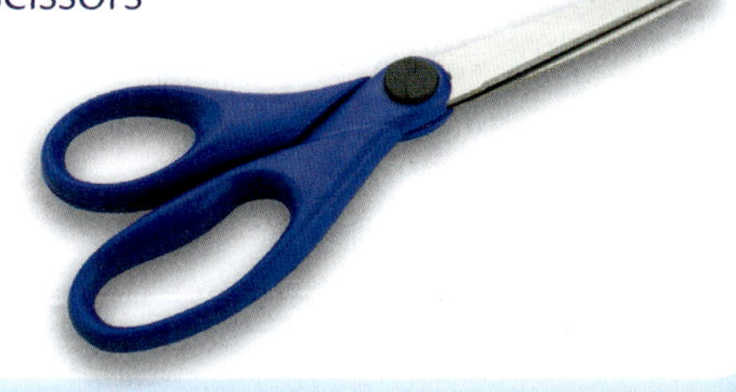

Steps

1. Lay some newspaper on your work space to protect the surface. Spread one sheet of baking paper on top of the newspaper.
2. Choose two or three wax crayons and peel off the paper. Any bright colours will be suitable.

3. Using the grater, carefully grate some of each wax crayon over the baking paper. Move the grater around so that the shavings are evenly spread across the paper. Just a light sprinkling of wax shavings is needed – if you grate too much, the wax will be too thick.

4. Take the other sheet of baking paper and place it over the wax shavings, so that the shavings are sandwiched between the two sheets of baking paper.

5. Ask an adult to do the next step for you. Heat an iron until it is warm, and run it over the baking paper until the wax starts to melt and spread. Make sure that all the wax has melted, especially at the edges, so that the two sheets of baking paper are stuck together. Then, set the paper aside to cool.

6. While the paper cools, take the small bowl and place it on the piece of cardboard. Trace around the bowl with one of the crayons, to draw a circle. Cut out the circle with the scissors.

7. Once the baking paper has cooled completely, check that the two sheets are properly stuck together. If they seem loose, use some glue to stick the edges together.

8. Use the scissors to cut the baking paper into two long strips. One strip should be very wide, about 25 cm, as this will be the body of the lantern. The other strip should be about 5 cm wide, to make a handle for the lantern.

9. Take the larger rectangle of baking paper and cut a zigzag line down one of the long sides. It should look like a line of sharp teeth.

10. Wrap the baking paper around the bowl from Step 6, to make a **cylinder** shape. Make sure the zigzag edge is at the top of the cylinder.

11. Staple the top and bottom of the cylinder to hold it together.

12. Fold the "teeth" down and put a drop of glue on each of them. Place the cardboard circle onto the ring of "teeth".

13. Turn the cylinder upside down and place the bowl back inside it. The weight of the bowl will press down on the glue, to help the baking paper stick to the cardboard. Then, leave your new lantern to dry.

14. Take the smaller strip of baking paper to make a handle for the lantern. Staple one end of the strip to the open end of the lantern.

    Bend the strip over, and staple the other end to the opposite side of the lantern.

15. Once the glue is dry, take the bowl out of your lantern and replace it with the LED tealight candle.

16. Go somewhere dark and turn on the light inside your lantern. **Observe** how the light makes the melted wax glow!

A Colourful Sun Catcher

Sun catchers are small pieces of art, mostly made from coloured glass. They are hung in windows, and are designed to reflect sunlight and create patterns in a room. Not all sun catchers are made from glass. In this activity, the sun catcher is made from white glue and coloured beads and buttons.

Goal

To make a sun catcher

Materials

You will need:

a few sheets of newspaper

a plastic lid from a jar

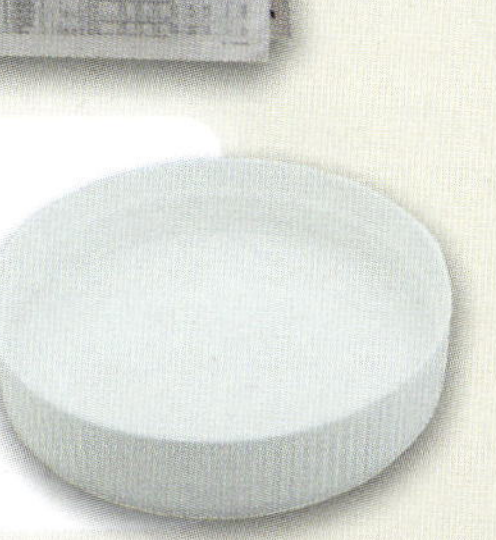

PVA glue

a small ball of plasticine

an **assortment** of small, coloured plastic beads or buttons, or similar objects

a skewer

a piece of string, about 30 cm long.

scissors

Steps

1. Lay some newspaper on your work space to protect the surface. Place the lid upside down on top of the newspaper.
2. Carefully pour some of the glue into the lid. Make sure the bottom of the lid is completely covered with glue.

3. Place your coloured plastic objects into the wet glue. Make sure they are spread out and cover most of the lid.

4. Leave the lid in a warm, sunny place to dry. This will take a few days.

5. When the glue feels hard and has started to become clear, carefully peel it from the lid. If the glue is still wet on the back, turn it over so the wet side is facing up, and leave it until it is thoroughly dry.

6. When the glue is completely dry, trim the rough edges of the circle of dried glue with scissors.

7. Roll some plasticine into a ball, so it is about the size of a large marble. Place the ball of plasticine under the edge of your sun catcher, where you would like the top to be. Carefully use the skewer to make a hole in the top of your sun catcher. Push the skewer through the hard glue and into the plasticine beneath.

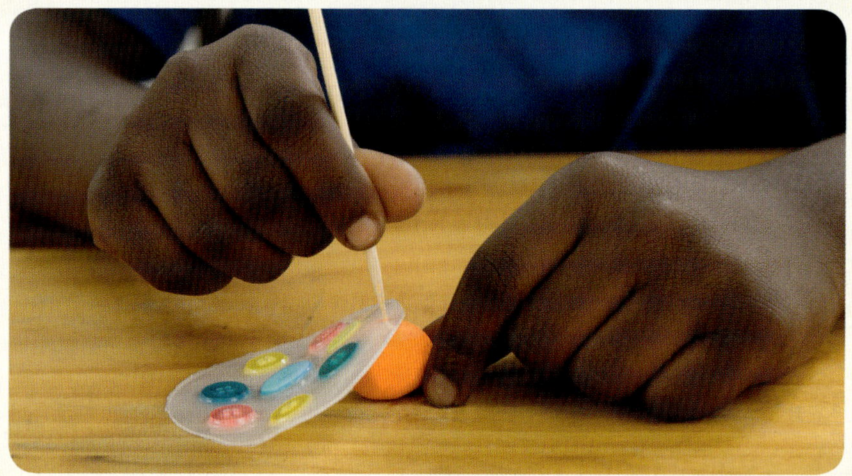

8. Thread the string through the hole. Tie a knot close to the top of the sun catcher, to hold it in place.

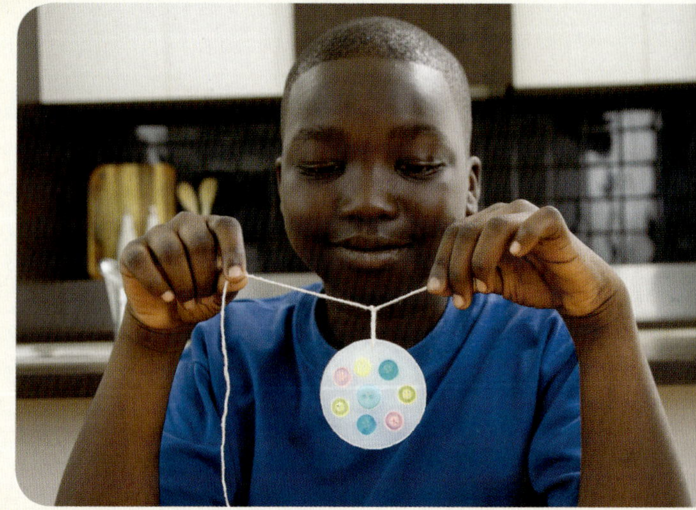

9. Hang your new sun catcher on a window that receives lots of sunlight. Observe the colourful patterns it creates when it catches the sun.

Coloured Sun Catchers

Sun catchers do not have to be circular or white. To make a colourful sun catcher, use water-based markers to colour the inside of the lid before pouring in the PVA glue. Use just one or two colours. Pour the glue into the lid and follow the steps described previously. As the glue dries, the colour from the marker will blend with the glue to change the colour of your sun catcher!

Sun Catchers in Different Shapes

There are two ways to make a sun catcher of a different shape. When the PVA glue has dried, use the scissors to cut another shape instead of a circle. It could be a diamond, a square or even a star. Decide what shape to make before starting, so that the beads and buttons can be placed in the right positions. Or, use old cookie cutters instead of lids, to create different-shaped sun catchers. When using cookie cutters, place them onto baking paper before pouring the PVA glue.

Constellation Names and Pictures

Long ago, people looked up at the stars and imagined that they formed pictures, such as bulls, dogs and other figures. These groups of stars are called **constellations**.

Goal

To make a constellation name and **portrait**

Materials

You will need:

sheets of A4 black paper

a sheet of craft foam or a folded tea towel

a light-coloured crayon or pencil

a skewer.

Steps to Make a Constellation Name

1. Use the crayon or pencil to write a name on the black paper. Make the letters large enough, so that they fill the paper.

2. Place the craft foam or folded tea towel under the black paper.

3. Make holes in the paper along the lines in the name, by pushing the skewer through the paper and into the foam or tea towel underneath. Twist the skewer slightly to create a neat hole. Do not make the holes too close together, as the paper could tear.

4. Once you have finished tracing one or two of the letters, hold the paper up to a light, to see if the letters can be read clearly.

5. Place the paper back onto the foam or tea towel and use the skewer to complete the rest of the letters. Then, add some extra holes around the name. Do not try to make any patterns, but instead try to place the holes in random positions. They should look like a **galaxy** of stars.
6. Place the completed work in a sunny window and admire the beautiful stars!

Steps to Make a Constellation Portrait

1. Use the crayon or pencil to draw a simple portrait on the black paper. Draw from the shoulders up and keep the portrait simple. The fewer lines the better. Sign your work when the drawing is complete.

2. Place the craft foam or folded tea towel under the black paper.

3. Make holes in the paper along the lines in the drawing, by pushing the skewer through the paper and into the foam or tea towel underneath. Twist the stick slightly to create a neat hole. Do not make the holes too close together, as the paper could tear.

4. Once you have finished tracing part of the drawing, hold the paper up to a light, to see if the portrait can be seen clearly.

5. Place the paper back onto the foam or tea towel and use the skewer to complete the rest of the lines of the drawing. Don't forget to include your name!
6. To create the effect that the portrait is made from stars, make lots of extra holes around the outside of the drawing.

7. Place the portrait in a sunny window and **admire** the face among the stars!

Glossary

admire *(verb)*	to enjoy looking at something
assortment *(noun)*	a group of similar things that are different sizes or colours
constellations *(noun)*	groups of stars
cylinder *(noun)*	a shape like a tube with two flat, circular ends
galaxy *(noun)*	a system of stars, gas and dust held together by gravity
navigate *(verb)*	to work out the right direction to go
observe *(verb)*	to watch carefully
portrait *(noun)*	a picture of a person, usually of their face